The Royal Tour of Canada

The 1939 Visit of
King George VI and Queen Elizabeth

Copyright © 2002 Lynx Images Inc.
Copyright © text 2002 RB Fleming

Published by Lynx Images Inc.
P.O. Box 5961, Station A
Toronto, Canada M5W 1P4
Web Site: http://www.lynximages.com

1st Edition: June 2002

Project Producers: Russell Floren, Barbara Chisholm and Andrea Gutsche
Cover and inside design: Andrea Gutsche, Lynx Images Inc.

Front Cover left: Children in Victoria practise waving their flags in preparation for the Royal Visit. —National Archives PA-209862

Front Cover right: The Royal Couple stand under the Peace Tower, Parliament Hill, Ottawa —*Star Weekly*, 30 June 1939

Back Cover: The King and Queen arrive at the New Brunswick Legislative Building in Fredericton. —National Archives PA-209862

National Library of Canada Cataloguing in Publication

Fleming, Rae Bruce, 1944-
        The royal tour of Canada : the 1939 visit of King George VI and Queen Elizabeth / R.B. Fleming.

Includes index.
ISBN 1-894073-37-1

        1. George VI, King of Great Britain, 1895-1952--Journeys--Canada--Pictorial works. 2. Elizabeth, Queen, consort of George VI of Great Britain, 1900- --Journeys--Canada--Pictorial works. 3. Visits of state--Canada--1939--Pictorial works. I. Title.

FC223.R6 1939 F54 2002   971.063'2   C2002-902532-X
F1034.F54 2002

The Royal Tour of Canada

The 1939 Visit of King George VI
and Queen Elizabeth

by RB Fleming

LYNX
IMAGES

Like Old Friends

By the time King George and Queen Elizabeth reached Ottawa, the Queen and Mackenzie King confided in each other like old friends. She was sometimes forthright in her opinions, and probably did not realize that the Prime Minister recorded all their conversations each evening in his diary.

Preface

───✦───

There are already several books on royalty in Canada. So why this one? Up to this point, studies of the Royal Tour of 1939 have examined what Canadians and Newfoundlanders (in 1939, Newfoundland was a Crown colony, separate from Canada) saw in May and June 1939. In other words, previous studies have focussed on King George VI and Queen Elizabeth. This book alters that point of view. Thanks to an exciting discovery of photographs stored for decades at the National Archives of Canada, this book is able to add a hitherto overlooked dimension of the tour: Canadians themselves. It recasts the story of the tour from the vantage point of the spectators. Never before had our ancestors posed for so many cameras at any one time. Nor, as a matter of fact, ever since. In other words, this book is a new way of looking at royal tours.

To provide context for the photographs, I consulted both published and unpublished documents, including the diaries of Prime Minister Mackenzie King, which historians usually treat less seriously than have I. No one else, to my knowledge, reported so consistently the intimate details of conversations and events. His dreams and visions in no way diminish his important role as an articulate eyewitness.

Government sources such as the Papers of the Secretary of State and of the Governor General provide details of the minute planning for the tour. Gustave Lanctot's *The Royal Tour of King George VI and Queen Elizabeth in Canada and the United States of America: 1939* is indispensable. Like Mackenzie King, Lanctot accompanied the King and Queen across the country. Though more discreet than the Prime Minister, he was no less an acute observer and recorder.

The work of David Cannadine, especially his *Ornamentalism*, is always illuminating. Interpretations of the Crown in Canada, as well as biographies of King George VI and Queen Elizabeth, The Queen Mother, explain their various roles. Especially helpful were *The Queen Behind The Throne* by Michael De-la-Noy and Sara Bradford's *The Reluctant King*. Kenneth Munro's essays on Canada and the Crown are always perceptive and informative, as is *The Rise and Fall of the British Empire* by Lawrence James.

Several people helped in other ways. Elizabeth Richardson and Kathy Hooke lent collections of press clippings and books. Kathleen Bowley and Alan Lindsay clarified short forms and colloquialisms. Ian Campbell let me see invitations to events in Ottawa. At the National Archives, Jean Matheson solved photograph identification problems, and Andrew Rodger played the tireless and helpful archivist to perfection. It was he who pointed me to the large collection of unaccessioned tour photographs, for which he has my endless thanks. In London, Sir Alistair Aird, Private Secretary to the Queen Mother, confirmed that yes, indeed, she still thought of the Royal Tour of 1939 as a highlight of her life.

Kenneth Munro, Munroe Scott, Ronald Rees, Diana Rees and Will Ferguson accentuated strengths and pointed out weaknesses in my drafts. (Any remaining flaws are mine alone.) I thank Will Ferguson for his comments, printed on the back cover. Eric Wrate copied some photographs; Arthur Boustead, Garry Toffoli, Ronald Rees, Ken Alsop, Eleanor Parliament, Kenneth Munro, Joan Banks, Donald Smith, Michael Filey, Lilianne Plamondon, Richard Jones and J.L. Grantatstein identified photographs. I consulted several people who witnessed the tour or who had relatives who did so: Joan Banks, John Edwards, Herb Furniss, Richard Jones, Neysa Mitchell, Lilianne Plamondon, Marjorie Porter, Munroe Scott, Joan Macdonald, Paul Hellyer, James McKee, Edward Smith Ida Johns, Carol Stoddard, Jarvis Stoddard and Percy Steele.

I am grateful that Paul Litt put me in touch with Lynx Images, whose delightful and talented principals, Russell Floren, Barbara J. Chisholm and Andrea Gutsche, made working on this project a pleasure. I also want to thank Barbara D. Chisholm and Amy Harkness for their assistance in copy editing and proofing.

May I dedicate this book to all who saw the tour, to those of us who wish we had seen it, and to the Queen of 1939, who recently embarked on the grandest tour of all.

R.B. Fleming, Argyle, Ontario, May 2002

At the Legislature
King George and Queen Elizabeth visit the New Brunswick Legislative Building in Fredericton on June 13th.

A Serious Moment
In Victoria on May 30th, the Royal Couple sign one of the many guest books on the tour.

Crowd Control

June 14th. The Mounties may always get their man, but enthusiastic crowds like these Maritimers at Cape Tormentine, N.B., are sometimes difficult to control.

The Royal Tour of Canada 1939

⟡

T he night before the King and Queen arrived in Canada, Prime Minister Mackenzie King had a dream. In it, he was talking to King George V, and either Queen Alexandra or Queen Mary who were all "extremely kind, indeed affectionate," he confided to his diary. The vision, he thought, was a good omen. The tour of King George VI and Queen Elizabeth across Canada and to Newfoundland would be a success.

Neither Mackenzie King nor anyone else could have predicted how successful the Royal Tour of 1939 would be, nor how indelible its memory would remain today. The tour was one of a handful of events that remain etched in our nation's memory. This was, after all, the first time that a reigning sovereign had set foot on Canadian soil. For the King and Queen, the tour was an important test, both personally and as the embodiment of the monarchy. For Great Britain, the tour was a weather vane, indicating the direction in which Canadian loyalty to the Mother Country was blowing. The tour has been credited with turning "O Canada" into our national anthem. More Canadians posed for more cameras than at any other time in our history. But above all, the Royal Tour began a month of celebration that, for the first time ever, united Canadians from coast to coast.

Not surprisingly, many Canadians today, even those so young that they had to be held up on a parent's shoulders, recall not only where they saw the King and Queen, but even on which street, or from which storey of a particular building. Today in Québec City, Jeannette Bussières still recalls the enthusiasm of the crowds who came out to see the Royal Couple on the morning of Thursday, May 18th, at Pont-Rouge between Québec and Trois-Rivières. In Ottawa the next day, twelve-year-old Munroe Scott saw the King and Queen as they were

Place d'Armes

The royal procession passes in front of Notre Dame Cathedral in Montréal on May 18th. Over a million people lined the route.

driven through Confederation Square in an open landau. Young Scott stood in his scout uniform near Union Station. The memory is unforgettable, though today the novelist and playwright does confess that he was more impressed by the Royal Canadian Dragoons with their gleaming breastplates and helmets, and even more so by the scarlet-coated Mounties. In Toronto, eighteen-year-old Neysa Mitchell, along with her parents and her new husband, Charles, had a splendid view of the King and Queen as they greeted veterans outside the Christie Street Military Hospital on Monday, May 22nd. Neysa's father, Russell Copp, who worked for Eaton's, had arranged a spot at a large window of the company warehouse across the street. Percy Steele was only six at the time, but today he even remembers the colour and make of car (a green '29 Chev, driven by Mel Bishop) that took him to Toronto to see the King and Queen at Union Station. A week later in sunny Vancouver, Joan Macdonald saw the Royal Couple several times. Though at first reluctant to battle the crowds, her father, Fergus, was so smitten by the beauty of the Queen when he first saw her on Point Grey Road that he jumped into his car and drove his wife and two daughters to several other viewing spots, including the Seaforth Armouries. Even people who saw nothing more than the dazzling train—royal blue with silver and gold decorations—as it sped toward its next rendezvous, recall the exact railway crossing where they stood and waved at the invisible Royal Couple.

Across the country, there are thousands of similar stories. As a signpost marking our private journeys, for many Canadians the Royal Tour ranks with the assassination of President Kennedy, the outbreak and conclusion of the two World Wars and that glorious day in 1972 when Paul Henderson scored the winning goal for Canada.

Requests to Meet Them

Long before the King and Queen arrived in Canada, Canadians from coast to coast had become excited. During the months of planning, requests to meet Their Majesties poured into Ottawa. From the Mother Superior of le Couvent Jésus-Marie de Sillery came an offer *"en hommage à sa Majesté, pour la nuit qu'Elle passera à Québec, un amueblement royal exécuté et sculpté en 1860...."* The bedroom suite, five pieces in black oak, had been made especially for the visit of the Prince of Wales, the King's grandfather, during his visit to Canada in 1860. The Mother Superior hoped that King George would use it while in Québec City.

Organizations such as the War Amputees, l'Association Canadienne-Française d'Education de l'Ontario, the Australian-New Zealand Club of Toronto and the British and Foreign Bible Society in Canada and Newfoundland begged for permission to make presentations and addresses. From the Bricklayers, Masons and Plasterers' International Union came a request that the Queen, who was to lay the cornerstone of the Supreme Court Building, be made an honourary member. A.S. Redfern, private secretary to the governor general,

Sherbrooke Welcomes Their Majesties

On June 12th, 125,000 residents of Sherbrooke, Québec, cheered Their Majesties in English and French upon their return to Canada from the United States. To the right of the Queen, Margaret Armitage, daughter of the mayor of Sherbrooke, has just presented a bouquet. On her left is Monseigneur Desraleau, Bishop of Sherbrooke. A veteran stands in front of the King.

Montreal
Que.

Rt. Hon. W. L.
Mackenzie King;

Dear Sir;
I am writting
you to see if you
can arrange for me
to sing and act for
our beloved King and
Queen when they visit
our fine city, Ottawa.
I am a boy 9 years of age
born in Ottawa. I
have been studying
down in New York
and now I am in
Montreal. The M.G.M.
Company are going
to take me to Holly-

SOUVENIR O...

sniffed that he saw no more need for the Queen to be made a plasterer than to be appointed a judge.

Linda Harris of Ottawa wanted to present the King and Queen with a table made from an elm tree grown on the Queen's family's estate at Glamis. One man thought that maple syrup would make an appropriate gift, while young Norman Thorp, a rising star from Montréal, offered to sing. Hugh Keenleyside, Secretary of the Interdepartmental Committee for the Royal Visit, turned him down, as he did most requests, including several from lacrosse and baseball associations requesting the presence of the King and Queen at their games. An "Irish Soldier Poet" who was a Canadian veteran of the Great War, and author of a collection of poetry called "Rhymes of an Old War Horse," was vexed that he had not received a special invitation to read his poem "Welcome" to Their Majesties. One Member of Parliament from Toronto asked that his "very brilliant niece" accompany him to various functions.

Small wonder that A.S. Redfern created a "Book of Queer Proposals," also known as a "Book of

I Want to Sing

A letter from Norman Thorp requesting to sing for the King and Queen. (Inset) Young Norman Thorp from Montreal.

Horrors." If all offers had been accepted, the King and Queen would have spent the war years in Canada.

A more serious request came from Le Comité permanent des Congrès de la Langue Française en Amérique, which, along with la Société St-Jean-Baptiste, requested that official functions, such as the laying of the cornerstone of the Supreme Court Building, be performed in French as well as English. Although press releases were usually sent out in both languages, the Dominion Government and the City of Ottawa, by and large, functioned in one language in 1939. However, both the Queen and the King were proficient in French, and the Queen's speech at the Supreme Court ceremony was delivered in both languages. At Québec City, the King had moved effortlessly from English to French, as he did in Ottawa and later in Halifax, to the great delight of newspapers such as *le Devoir*, which saw the speeches, broadcast live not only across Canada but also internationally, as affirmations of the bilingual nature of Canada.

The Camera Loves the Queen

The photographs included in this book tell us a great deal about ourselves in 1939, our attitudes to royalty

The Rituals of Monarchy
In Ottawa on May 19th, the Royal Couple pose for photographers under the Peace Tower after giving Royal Assent to Bills in the Senate.

and authority, our dress and our cities. The relationship of photography to government in the late 1930s, along with the power and limitations of the camera, are at the heart of these images. This was the first royal tour during which photographs taken in the morning could be viewed by authorities in the afternoon, then, after careful vetting, published in newspapers across Canada and abroad over the following days.

Into the Legislature

Victoria, May 30th. Ascending the steps of the Provincial Legislature Building are Premier and Mrs. Duff Patullo, the King and Queen, Lieutenant Governor and Mrs. Hamber and Prime Minister Mackenzie King.

Aboard the Pilot Train

Members of the press rode in the pilot train, which arrived half an hour ahead of the royal train. Among them were F.R. Daniel of the New York Times, Fred Griffin of the Star Weekly and R.V. Machel of The Daily Telegraph, London. Judith Robinson of the Toronto Globe was a thorn in the Prime Minister's side. (Below) Press and photographers' signatures.

These photographs were taken by professional photographers, many of whom worked for the Government of Canada. By the 1930s, the camera had become an arm and eye of governments and corporations, who for decades had been making visual records of their buildings, officials and official events. In 1919 the Dominion Government had established the Canadian Government Motion Picture Bureau (CGMPB) whose mandate was to record, by means of

moving and still pictures, the activities, property and personalities of the Dominion Government. The capital region as well as scenic spots across the country were also the subjects of the men who made up the CGMPB, which long preceded the better-known National Film Board (NFB), founded in 1939. Other photographers, representing media in Canada, Great Britain and the

United States, were also on the tour. Only rarely did they identify themselves. They "pooled" their images, and thus were known simply as the "pool." Across Canada and into the States, they travelled on an advance or "pilot" train. And because they arrived at train stations in advance, they had time to set up their cameras. While waiting for the royal train, they took pictures of the crowds, the police escorts, and themselves. When the royal train arrived, the attention of the cameras shifted to royalty. Although there were precedents, such as *50,000 Miles with the Prince of Wales*, a documentary premiered in 1925, this tour was the most carefully recorded of all royal tours.

The Queen long understood film. Her love affair with the camera dated from those winsome photographic portraits of the young Elizabeth Bowes-Lyon during the first decade of the 20th century. The camera followed her into the 1920s when she married into the Royal Family. In the 1930s she used the camera to promote the idea of the happy family. By 1939, she was mistress of the pose that seemed to ignore the camera, still or moving. She loved the camera so much that she seemed to flirt with it. She had an easy manner, she moved gracefully, important especially for moving pictures, and quite clearly she enjoyed the company of cameramen. They returned that affection by presenting

Making News
At the Banff Springs Hotel on May 27th, cameraman Roy Tash of the CGMPB films the King and Queen, along with Mackenzie King, after they had just given a "photo op" on the terrace.

her in the most appealing manner possible. Her combination of majesty and the common touch comes through in almost every camera angle.

And though she had begun her film "career" during the days of silent movies (in newsreels and the film of the Coronation of 1937, she did not speak), her warm, mezzo voice, along with an unobtrusive Mayfair accent, worked well in "talkies," and thus enhanced her appeal. (The King's hesitant voice, on the other hand, made listeners nervous. As for Mackenzie King, he never did learn that in movies, there is no need to pontificate. Neither man looked entirely comfortable in either moving or still pictures.) The Queen did not even mind redoing a scene. During the Supreme Court ceremonies

The Boisterous West

At the Regina Exhibition Grounds on May 25th, chronicler Gustave Lanctot reported that "Indians of four tribes... chanted and danced ...in a ceremonial that proclaimed the King a Pipe Chief." He added that "there were folk singers in national costumes and blues singers in cowboy hats, as well as hot-dog stands and a corral of Indian ponies."

By 1939, she was a professional. In Washington, the Prime Minister and Mrs. John D. Rockefeller noted the Queen's movie star quality. Wallis Simpson called her Shirley Temple, which suggests that Mrs. S. also saw the movie star in the Queen (and was no doubt envious because she herself appeared pinched in photographs, newsreels and home movies). In person and on film, Elizabeth played the Queen, a role that combined her own charming personality with the duties of monarchy. She became so adept at using the camera, especially during the war, that Hitler, no mean cinematic *artiste* himself, called her Germany's most dangerous enemy.

The 1939 tour used the latest in cameras and developing techniques. The pilot train had a laboratory that could develop and print photographs and films within a few hours. Along the route, and especially in scenic and less busy places such as Banff and Jasper, the King enthusiastically took his own moving pictures. On June 1st, thanks to the developing lab on the train, he was able to splice

on May 20th, she said "I declare this stone to be well and truly laid." It did not carry over the radio, and thus was not recorded for the voice track of the moving film. The Prime Minister asked her if she would move closer to microphones, and repeat the line. She was happy to oblige.

together over 700 feet of film, which he then ran through a projector. The Queen had a still camera, which she used from time to time.

Why were the King and Queen so willing to cooperate with the cameramen? By 1939, the Palace and the Royal Family had perfected the ritualistic side of monarchy. From the 1880s to the Great War, as its real power declined, it had reinvented itself and its "traditions" in order to enhance its symbolic powers as the embodiment of the British Nation and the Empire. What was missing, however, was rapport. Few previous members of the Royal Family had been capable of relating to the millions of ordinary subjects. For most royals, smiling was painful. While enjoying pageantry, the camera also loves a star with an easy manner and a smile. Queen Elizabeth's important role was to humanize royalty. In pre-television days, still and moving pictures were the most effective way of projecting that humanity and warmth to the millions of people throughout the Empire, and in the USA. The popularity of the Royal Couple as seen in newsreels (which gave cinema audiences ten or fifteen minutes of news prior to the main feature) finally convinced the Establishment and people at home (who also observed the Canadian tour in their press and cinemas) that George and Elizabeth were perfect for the role of King and Queen.

In 1939, it was still possible for royals and political leaders to control the creation of appropriate images. If Mackenzie King couldn't get exactly the image he wanted, he simply ordered editing or airbrushing. In that, he joined both Hitler and Stalin, who were in the habit of airbrushing out unwanted faces. The Queen herself had photographer Cecil Beaton retouch photographic portraits taken soon after her return from Canada. In 1939, photographers had to seek official approval before setting up cameras or before asking the King and Queen to adopt a pose or to change position. They were not allowed to come within twenty feet of the Royal Couple, nor were they to use flash bulbs during royal speeches.

Although from time to time the press and photographers had to be "bought off" by means of "photo ops," particularly at Banff where the King and Queen wanted several unrecorded hours of rest and walks, most of the media of 1939 reflected the mood of Canadians—they were enthusiastic yet deferential. Greg Clark of the *Toronto Star*, Jacques Girouard of *la Presse* and Bruce Hutchison of the *Vancouver Sun* wrote glowing reports, as did Bruce West of *The Globe and Mail*, whose description of the brief stop at Trois-Rivières on May 18th sounds overly decorous today. "In both French and English," West wrote, "the words of praise

"A Note of Splendour"

Crowds pass the Empress Hotel after ceremonies at the Legislature Building on May 30th. "Victoria has left the most pleasing of all impressions," noted Mackenzie King, "a note of splendour at...the beginning of the return way."

and the pledges of loyalty are flying about the town like sparks in the wake of some fire of patriotism set off by the wave of the hands and the quick, friendly smiles of the youthful Sovereign and his Queen."

Canadians—Long-Time Monarchists

The enthusiasm of the crowds, and journalists, can be attributed to the fact that it was the first time that a reigning Sovereign had set foot on Canadian soil. It was not, of course, the first time a member of royalty had visited or lived in Canada. In order to unify the Empire and to create in Canada what David Cannadine calls the hierarchical and Gothic society of England, relatives of Queen Victoria had come and gone, her father in the late 18th century, followed by numerous children and grandchildren.

Long before Queen Victoria's father set foot on Canadian soil, monarchies had played a significant role in the exploration, settlement and development of Canada. In 1497, John Cabot's explorations were sponsored by Henry VII; and under the aegis of Henri IV, Québec was founded in 1608. In the early 1700s, the King of France paid half the costs of Montréal's fortifications; in the 1760s, George III helped to

"Here is Your King"

In the domed rotunda of Union Station, Winnipeg, on June 4th, the Queen greets veterans of Deer Lodge. She was so moved by the blind Sergeant Fletcher, a veteran of South Africa and WWI, that all she could do was hold his hand. When the King came by, she passed Fletcher's hand to him with the words "Here is your King."

rebuild part of Montréal destroyed by fire. Royalty provided funds for cleaning up the Plains of Abraham for the Québec Tricentenary of 1908. As Soldiers of the King, we have fought wars for King/Queen and Country. In the name of the Crown, vast amounts of land were deeded to fur trade and railway companies, and to settlers and homesteaders. Soldiers, notably the Royal North West Mounted Police, forerunner of the Royal Canadian Mounted Police, and politicians, often knighted by the Crown, helped to open up lands for settlement. It was a royal act that guaranteed to French Canadians their language, law and religion. Even when Great Britain itself was experiencing pangs of republicanism in the 1870s, Canadians remained loyal.

The affection and respect for monarchy and its representatives in Canada can be seen in the names we have bestowed on ourselves—some of them, admittedly, imposed by officials representing the Crown, but most chosen voluntarily. These names include two provinces, innumerable villages, towns and cities, including Montréal, Regina and Victoria; counties and townships; streets, squares and gates, from Place Royale to Terrace Dufferin and the Princes' Gates, not to mention innumerable King and Queen Streets; and hotels and theatres. Especially in given names, from Kent, King and Lorne to Réal, Reine-Victoria and Louise, have Canadians demonstrated loyalty. The term "royal" affixed to clubs bestowed prestige.

*Great
Anticipation*
*On June 2nd,
Edmonton children
sit on an iron fence
while women keep
watch.*

By and large, royalty was an easy sell to most Canadians of British ancestry (including even Highland Scots and Irish dissidents). To a lesser extent, it was accepted by those who continued to speak the language of Molière and Louis XIV. But what about the increasingly ethnic fabric of Canada, which developed well after royal place names were affixed to maps? In addition to the care taken to include French Canada and First Nations, the tour noted the fact that Canada in 1939 was a multicultural country, at least unofficially. As Canada welcomed immigrants from outside the English- or French-speaking world, a process that had begun in earnest during the late 19th century, the question of integration and loyalty became paramount.

How to include these newcomers and their children in one great Canadian family under the monarchy? The photographs in this book show that all varieties of Canadians participated in the tour. The tour also succeeded in modifying entrenched attitudes on the part of long-established Canadians. Geoffrey Hewelcke of the *Montréal Standard*, reporting from Melville, Saskatchewan, on June 3rd, promised that never again would he assume that "foreigners" born in the Ukraine, Germany, Slovakia or Sweden, who were giving the King and Queen as enthusiastic a welcome as anyone else on the Prairies, were not good Canadian citizens. It would take time for the majority of Canadians to appreciate ethnic diversity, but some forty years later, Sylvia

Fedoruk, one of the Ukrainian-Canadian children watching that day in Melville, was appointed Lieutenant-Governor of her province and Chancellor of the University of Saskatchewan.

In 1939, the impression was thus successfully created that Canada could turn people from around the world into good British subjects. Even those who had rebelled against the hierarchical status quo of Canadian and Imperial society were co-opted, or so the tour made it seem. In Saskatoon, the King and Queen shook hands with Thomas Swain, a Métis veteran of the Rebellion of 1885. The mayor of Winnipeg, John Queen, who welcomed the King and Queen to his city, had been thrown in jail for participating in the Winnipeg General Strike of 1919. Very early in the tour, the Royal Couple learned that the grandfathers of the two most prominent officials to greet them had once rebelled against the Crown. At Québec, the Prime Minister announced that both he and Senator Raoul Dandurand were descended from men who had participated in the political rebellions of the 1830s. A few days later at Laurier House, his residence in Ottawa, Mackenzie King proudly showed the Royal Couple photographs of his mother and her father, the rebel leader William Lyon Mackenzie, along with the proclamation, issued in the name of Queen Victoria, for his arrest. The country, it

Highest Point
On June 1st, a young girl awaits King George and Queen Elizabeth at Mount Robson, B.C.

seemed, had the amazing ability of settling political disturbances in such a way that the descendants of rebels could become leaders a century later, and a man considered an enemy of the state could become one of its mayors just a couple of decades later.

Canadians of all ranks came out to see the parade. The higher the rank, the deeper the bow and curtsey. Throughout the spring of 1939, thousands of women practised in front of mirrors and relatives. A few photographs in this book remind one of Prime Minister Alexander Mackenzie's description, as reported in P.B. Waite's *Arduous Destiny*, of two large society women who in 1879 curtsied so dramatically before Governor

General Lord Lorne and Princess Louise that people seated immediately behind feared personal injury if the curtsey failed during recovery.

Draped in furs, the wives of lieutenant governors, mayors and cabinet ministers often gave the impression that the animals of northern Canada had been slaughtered beyond regeneration. Ordinary Canadians, less aware of the niceties of protocol, were happy to chat with George and Elizabeth. In Savona, British Columbia, Grannie Villiers, one of the oldest members of the community, led a spontaneous rendition of "God Save the King" on her fiddle, and Herbie Wilson, a schoolboy, shouted "So long, Your Majesties!" as the train pulled away after a brief water stop. During another brief stop in B.C., fifty people broke into "God Save the King," then someone suggested "O Canada." The King asked who would start. "You lead it, mister," shouted a small boy to the King. For the tour, even though they had been moved to the periphery of Empire by the settlement process, Natives donned their finest ceremonial attire. In Edmonton, they sang "God Save the King" in Cree.

The timing of the tour, as it turned out, was perfect. For almost a decade, Canadians had been experiencing the worst economic depression ever. Some smaller cities and towns did not even have the funds for street decorations, and the clothing in many photographs was probably the only good suit or dress available. There was also the threat of another war. Many in the cheering crowds had bleak memories of fathers and brothers and husbands, some of whom had returned in 1919 with body and spirit so maimed that they had to be tucked away in veterans' hospitals forever. Some 60,000 Canadians never returned, their bodies absorbed by the mud of Vimy Ridge and Flanders Fields. The cameras thus recorded Canadians whose joyful enthusiasm masked the fears and anxieties engendered by those 20th-century economic and military cataclysms.

The Tour Made Them

For Britain, Canada's support and enthusiasm were vital. The tour was a way of testing the waters for the next war. During the planning of the tour, which began soon after the Coronation of 1937, it was becoming obvious that Hitler and Mussolini had expansion in mind. In March 1939, Hitler had occupied part of Czechoslovakia, and in April, Mussolini invaded Albania. More than ever, imperial solidarity was important. Could Canada be counted on to help Britain if Hitler expanded beyond the limits set by Britain's policy of Appeasement? Like the other Dominions, Canada had been loosening ties with Britain. In 1919, Mackenzie King had done away with titles for Canadians. In 1922, Canada had let it be known that her Parliament alone would decide on entry into war. Since the Treaty of Westminster of 1931, the "White Dominions" (a term that then included South Africa!) controlled their own foreign policies. (The King and Queen were probably unaware that when the bells for the Peace Tower carillon, the same carillon that pealed forth welcomes in Ottawa, were being made in Croydon, England, in 1926, Mackenzie King had cried out "Equal Status!" as he threw a British halfpenny and a Canadian penny into the molten metal.)

For the King and Queen too, this tour was an important test, both personally and for the institution of the monarchy, which had come into disrepute during the abdication of Edward VIII in 1936. Did they have the fortitude and charisma to sustain a month-long tour?

Queen Elizabeth later claimed that Canada had made them, and that was true. The reception in Canada gave them self-confidence, especially the shy King George for whom public speaking was such an ordeal that his speeches were limited to five in number, and whose stammer was at times so apparent that officials sent word that no one was to mention the problem. (He

Unbridled Crowd
Windsor, Ontario, June 6th. Mounties have difficulty holding back the crowds as the Royal Couple stand on rear platform of train.

sometimes had difficulty with the "k" sound, and thus both "Québec" and "Canada" presented problems.) In the most unobtrusive manner, the Queen helped give the King the confidence to carry out the role that had been thrust upon him in 1936. During the tour, Alan Lascelles, the King's Acting Private Secretary, told the Prime Minister that while King George V used to laugh at his son's stammering, it was the Queen who "made him the man he is" by constantly encouraging him. The day after their return to London, even the great orator Winston Churchill noted the improvement in the King's self confidence and speaking ability.

Expressions of Loyalty

On May 17th, Premier Duplessis bows to the Queen outside the Château Frontenac prior to a state dinner hosted by the Québec Government. "Notre province a toujours été fidèle à la couronne britannique," *he announced earlier that day.*

The tour helped to establish this couple as the best representatives of the monarchy, and to banish even further the rival "court" of Edward, the Duke of Windsor, who remained popular in some quarters in Britain, the States and in Canada where he was seen as a victim of a high-handed English upper class. Before his abdication, he was perceived as a Prince and King of the "people."

The Canadian trip confirmed Elizabeth Bowes-Lyon as the royal with a common touch. She could effortlessly make small talk with ordinary Canadians in both official languages. Immediately after the cornerstone of the Supreme Court building was "well and truly laid," she kept a crowd of 70,000 waiting as she carried on a conversation in French with one of the masons; with one of the other two masons present, she talked about his native Scotland. Whether with children, their mothers, or even dogs, she found the right word. Among her favourite people were the war veterans, perhaps because she herself had lost a brother in France in 1915 and because she had also helped to entertain wounded soldiers at her home at Glamis.

Instinctively the Queen sensed what people were thinking. She had great listening skills, a trait not common to her imperious in-laws. Mackenzie King described her as "earnest," and he meant it as a compliment. She sensed that Mackenzie King, like her husband, was a man in need of encouragement. During her first day in Canada, she informed the Prime Minister that, like his ancestors, she was from Dundee and Aberdeen (while omitting the fact that the Earls of Strathmore were not quite from the same side of the tracks as Elizabeth Mackenzie and her son, William Lyon Mackenzie). When the Prime Minister felt ignored at the Windsor Hotel banquet in Montréal, the Queen sat him down beside her when they adjourned to an adjacent room. A few days later, she paid special attention to the photograph of his mother, along with a lock of her hair and wedding ring, at Laurier House.

While she enjoyed ordinary Canadians, she also knew royal protocol by heart. She loved the pageantry, the opening of Parliament, the Trooping of the Colour, the Coronation of 1937, and, of course, royal funerals, whose pomp and circumstance had largely developed only since the late 19th century. (She would have thoroughly enjoyed her own funeral, and by planning it in advance, in effect she did enjoy it!) She understood the quasi-religious character of the monarchy, that it embodied the hopes and dreams of people, and provided, in theory, at least, protection from the whims of legislators.

She was more intelligent than she let on. She was aware of the implications of the Statute of Westminster, and the enhanced role it gave the prime ministers of the Dominions. During the planning of the tour, the Prime Minister, on the one hand, and Alexander Hardinge at the Palace, along with Governor General Tweedsmuir on the other, differed as to the role of the Governor General of Canada. Mackenzie King insisted

An Informal Break

May 28th. King George and Queen Elizabeth move up from their rear car to board an auxiliary locomotive at Beavermouth, B.C., in preparation for the steep ascent of the Selkirk Mountains.

Crowds Gather

An energetic crowd gathers at the Stratford, Ontario, station on June 6th.

that the Constitution and Westminster made it the prime minister's right and duty to accompany the King and Queen as the King's constitutional advisor in Canada. As such, it was his right and duty to be the first to greet the King and Queen once they stepped onto Canadian soil. (He, of course, also had one eye on Canadian electors.) During lunch at the Banff Springs Hotel, the Queen told the Prime Minister that he indeed was correct, because the Statute of Westminster had settled all those questions.

Rarely are conversations with royalty reported, but at the end of each day, the Prime Minister recorded the day's discussions with the King and Queen. At the banquet at Government House on Friday evening, May 19th, Queen Elizabeth asked the Prime Minister what he thought of Hitler. She no doubt knew that Mackenzie King had visited Germany in 1937. He told her that he did not think that the German leader wanted war, and the Queen agreed. She continued to back Prime Minister Chamberlain's policy of Appeasement. She thought the problem was Joachim von Ribbentrop, and may have been surprised when the Prime Minister told her that the German Ambassador to London had once been a guest in the very room where they were dining. Even worse, in the Queen's estimation, was Max Aitken, Lord Beaverbrook (likely because of his newspapers' support for the Duke of Windsor during the abdication crisis). Beaverbrook, she thought, deserved the Tower. As well, Churchill was not the man to lead Great Britain, she told Mackenzie King, because he would only inflame the Germans. While the war changed her attitude to Churchill, though never to

Beaverbrook, it was obvious that the Queen had given some thought to the unstable European situation. She was one of the few Britons who had bothered to read Hitler's *Mein Kampf*. She was good at hiding her intelligence, as was the wont of women of her generation.

Logistics of the Tour

Although the photographs make the tour appear casual and informal, without much security, the papers of the Secretary of State and the Governor General prove just the opposite. Royals had always been targets of assassins. Archduke Ferdinand's death in 1914 is the best remembered today, but in 1934 the King of Yugoslavia, a Windsor relative, was assassinated in Paris. And so security plans in Canada were meticulous. The Governor General's office even prepared a list of "embarrassing people," a file that remains closed to this day. No civilian aircraft was allowed within three miles of the King and Queen. Niagara Falls and Windsor drew extra security because of "the rabid Irish element" in nearby Buffalo and Detroit. And, of course, the matter of preventing the Royal Couple from being crushed by crowds was a concern, especially since the Prince of Wales had been slightly injured by too much enthusiasm in 1919.

Four husky, red-coated Mounties, Sergeant Williams and Constables Langlois, Coughlin and Portelance, were assigned to keep close watch. From Scotland Yard came two private detectives, Messrs. Cameron and Giles, who in the photographs are identifiable by their pinstripes and their serious, searching looks. Eight other Mounties were on the Royal Train. In the pilot train, along with the photographers, was Chief Constable Canning from the United Kingdom. On the roofs of buildings, one can sometimes spy what appears to be an armed soldier standing beside a photographer, armed with a camera. One of the purposes of the pilot train was to ensure that the track was in good condition, free from any harmful devices.

Security did not come cheaply. By February 1939, the estimated cost of defence (naval, militia and air) to protect the Royal Couple amounted to just over $325,000, an astounding sum in a decade when "Brother Can You Spare a Dime" was a popular song. At each stop, local and provincial police forces, as well as RCMP, were called into service. Aircraft circled overhead. At twenty-six stopping places, almost 50,000 troops from the navy, militia and air services lined the routes.

At each stop, in addition to paid law officers, volunteers, often veterans and scouts, worked on crowd control. Even at each railway crossing—thousands of them—a local resident was assigned to keep watch, lest anyone try to commit suicide by hurling himself (or herself) in front of the trains. One such local official was Harry Furniss, north of Beaverton, Ontario, who was asked to watch a crossing that did not even exist, except on an old map of the Canadian Northern Ontario Railway. The concession line crossing the track, though planned, had never been constructed. Farm gates adjacent to the train tracks were wired shut.

The cost of the tour, aside from security, was also high. Transportation costs (trains, ships, destroyers and cars) were estimated at over $350,000, including $10,000 paid to General Motors of Canada for the use of two custom-built McLaughlin Buick sedans. (There were four cars in all, two from General Motors, and one each from Ford and Chrysler.) The cost of broadcasting speeches made by the King in Québec City, Ottawa, Winnipeg and Halifax was about $50,000. Rideau Hall expenses were estimated at $13,000, including $3,175 for the garden party, as well as a $1,000 dress allowance (!) for Lady Tweedsmuir. The Trooping of the Colour cost upwards of $20,000, and the unveiling of the War Memorial about $5,000.

The royal train itself consisted of twelve cars. The King and Queen were in the last two, Numbers One and Two. Number One, with a viewing balcony, had a sitting room, two bedrooms with dressing rooms and baths, in addition to two other bedrooms for staff. The second last car had a large lounge, kitchen, dining room for twelve, and a bedroom and office for Acting Secretary Alan

100,000 Montrealers Salute the King and Queen
On May 18th, a huge crowd gathers in Dominion Square to salute Their Majesties on the balcony of the Windsor Hotel. Afterwards, back in the hotel, a quartet sang "Alouette" as the Queen hummed the tune while making the appropriate gestures to nose, head and arms.

Lascelles. Wardrobe staff were also in car Number Two; Cameron and Giles of Scotland Yard were in the third car, which also housed a wardrobe and pressing room. In the next car was Brigadier W.T. Wood, Commissioner of the RCMP, followed by the car of the Prime Minister. In subsequent cars were a surgeon; a supply of maps; Gustave Lanctot, Dominion Archivist and official historian of the tour; telephone officers; a dining car; a baggage car; a telephone exchange; a generator; and more officials. The train was as well equipped as any first-class hotel. It was a rolling mini-palace.

No effort was spared to ensure the comfort of the King and Queen. His Majesty's favourite cigars and cigarettes were in good supply, along with 62 bottles of sherry, 42 bottles of cooking sherry (presumably for the chef); 60 bottles of whisky and 36 bottles of gin; 24 bottles of port, with smaller quantities of brandy, vermouth and Grand Marnier. (Without the occasional fortifying drink, the tour would have become unbearable.)

The royal suite was furnished with plenty of Canadian reading material, including Pauline Johnson's *Legends of Vancouver*, Stephen Leacock's *Sunshine Sketches of a Little Town*, E.C. Guillet's *Early Life in Upper Canada*, Louis Hémon's *Maria Chapdelaine*, George Wrong's *The Canadians*, J. Murray Gibbon's *Canadian Folk Songs, Old and New*, Bovey's *French Canadians Today*, and Kennedy's *The Constitution of Canada*, the latter no doubt a remedy for sleeplessness.

Au Revoir

At Halifax on June 15th, the Royal Couple bid farewell to their four Mountie escorts.

Union Jacks Held High

Children wait at Wainwright, Alberta, on June 3rd. For several years afterwards, school texts endeavoured to keep the Royal Tour fresh in the minds of children.

There was also a "Who's Who" of officials whom they were likely to meet, as well as large, detailed maps of Canada, with the route marked. The King, as his private secretary noted, was "very fond of maps." One map came in handy late one night when the train made an unscheduled stop at Savona, B.C., to take on water. In the pitch black of midnight, the bookshelves and maps of the brilliantly illuminated royal suite could clearly be seen through the open door. Tom Edwards, the local storekeeper, noted in his weekly newspaper column that the King, having been told the name of the place, returned to the suite and added it to his wall map.

What's Next For Canada?

The tour of 1939 confirmed that the monarchy had a role in the hearts and minds of people in the far-flung Dominions, and that this Royal Couple was the ideal pair to perpetuate the institution. When they left, Canadians missed them. A photograph of the departure from Halifax is rather moving. As massed pipers wail and plea "Will Ye No Come Back Again," a lone Mountie with his back to the camera watches the *Empress of Britain* pull away from Canada. What remained was an uncertain future. A lingering Depression? Another war? Canadians had spent more than a year anticipating and planning the visit. It came and went. Like the four Calgary women in the final scene of John Murrell's play *Waiting for the Parade*, our lives became merely ordinary again.

World War II brought Canada, at least the English-speaking part of it, even closer to the Mother Country and its King and Queen. The end of the war, however, made it clear that the old Empire of deference and rank was weakened beyond repair and that another Empire, brash and republican, had arisen immediately to the south, in whose shadow, like it or not, Canada was now living. And that new Empire had long ago rejected the old status-conscious Empire across the sea.

Paradoxically, the tour itself, designed to reinforce imperial unity, helped to create the idea of a Canadian nation. Thanks to the event itself, and to the almost instantaneous reproduction of images, Canadians caught daily glimpses of each other. In the age immediately before good roads, reliable motor cars, jet service, and television, the unimaginable distance between Victoria and Halifax was bridged by newspaper photographs, newsreels and live radio. "It will be easier for us," Greg Clark of the *Toronto Star* predicted, "to go where we are now going, now that we know we are all facing the one way." Without a doubt, noted the Prime Minister in Vancouver, the tour was helping "to make Canada a nation in the true sense of the word." The singing of "O Canada" across the country, both planned and spontaneous, suggested that Canadians were becoming conscious of themselves and their own country. In 1939, it was impossible to think of unity without monarchy and Empire. Eventually,

Motorcycle police and soldiers await the arrival of the King and Queen on May 23rd, along with citizens and officials.

however, nations acquire their own symbols and ornaments. In the long run, the folk song "O Canada" became our national anthem, replacing the hymn about protecting the monarch.

At the same time, the tour marked the beginning of the idea of a nation within a nation. The war that followed made evident the fissures that had always existed within Canada. Mayor Houde, who had so enthusiastically welcomed the King and Queen to Montréal, was jailed not a year later for recommending resistance to war service. In the late 1940s, Roger Lemelin's novel *les Plouffe* was

Caught in Mid-Stride

Beaverton, Ontario, June 6th. "... A man running. And no way now to know what happened then —none at all— unless, of course, you improvise."

—by Eavan Boland from a poem called "The Black Lace Fan my Mother Gave me" in the collection of poetry, Outside History. *Carcanet Press Limited* (1990).

published. Set in Québec City at the time of the Royal Tour, it paints a now defiant city in which Guillaume Plouffe throws a republican baseball across the hood of the royal car. This fictional protest can be understood in the aftermath of war and Conscription. In the late 1940s, French Canadians/Québécois were losing respect for the old order of Crown, Church and Anglo-Establishment. By 1960, the Quiet Revolution was in full leaf, and one of its principal voices was *le Devoir*, which now preached a sovereign Québec with one official language and one unofficial anthem called "Mon Pays."

In the 1970s and '80s, others within Canada were beginning to stir. The costumed Indians in this book were becoming the vociferous First Nations of the late 20th century, no longer willing to reaffirm unquestioned loyalty to a long-dead Queen, and now self-confident enough to destroy the Meech Lake Accord with the mere wave of a feather.

The star of the 1939 tour, Queen Elizabeth, born during the last months of Queen Victoria's reign, lived into the 21st century. What did not survive was the overwhelming affection and deference shown by our ancestors in these photographs. Much of the respect for authority and "tradition," and in particular the Monarchy, has been lost. There are many explanations for this change in attitude, including our own skepticism, an often hostile press and perhaps the fact that the grandchildren of the Queen of 1939 have not inherited enough of her sense of duty and her admirable ability to flirt without consequence. So long as Queen Elizabeth, the Queen Mother, lived, she was so respected and beloved that it would have been an insult to her person and to the institution she reinvented, represented and so skilfully perpetuated, to speak openly about choosing a different course.

Now that she is gone, the detractors of the monarchy will become bolder. The number of outspoken republicans is growing. Anthony de Palma, in *Here*, his study of North American free trade, argues that (English) Canadians maintain the monarchy only because our health plan and hand gun legislation alone would not sufficiently distinguish us from our American neighbours. In *Is Canada Trapped in a Time Warp?*, Randall White calls the monarchy archaic and obsolete. For Gen-Xers like author Will Ferguson, monarchy arrests Canada's evolution from colony to country. Journalists Jeffrey Simpson and Margaret Wente, and perhaps a majority of the French-language press, are also unsympathetic.

And the message of television, the medium that succeeded the movies and stills of 1939, is often unsympathetic to authority and tradition. The camera today is usually live and unedited, intrusive and unsympathetic. Who in 1939 could have imagined a picture of a Queen twisting the neck of a partridge? And of course the Prime Minister of 1939 would never have considered performing a pirouette in the presence of royalty, even if he had been capable of doing so.

Today the monarchy, especially one based in a distant capital, is difficult to defend. So much relies on suspension of disbelief and the luck of genes. However, a habit so strongly ingrained over centuries will not be easy to break. And to take its place, what are the options? A smaller version of the United States? Will we not grow weary of commissions, royal or otherwise, that will decide our constitutional future? And a combination of medicare and long winters is not likely to bring out the excited crowds like those who came to see the parade of 1939.

In the meantime, let us enjoy these photographs of Canadians and their monarchs in May and June of 1939, that moment when royalty was king and Canadians were unabashed monarchists. May these photographs also serve as a reminder of a Queen we came to know and love, who for over sixty years reserved a special place in her heart for Canada and Canadians, not only because she received some of her warmest welcomes here but also because she never forgot that we helped her reinvent and modify the institution, as well as to confirm the shy, stammering George VI and his "earnest" Consort as the ideal couple to play the roles of King and Queen.

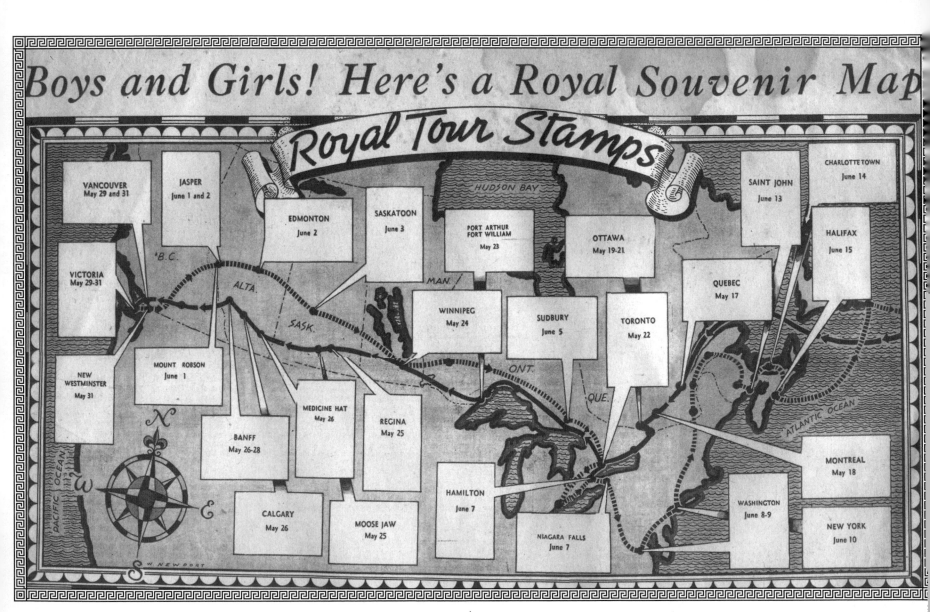

Souvenir Map
The *Star Weekly* encouraged children to follow the tour.

The Pilot Train
On May 21st, the pilot train pulls into Brockville, Ontario, half an hour before the royal train.

Riding the Engine
At Beavermouth, B.C., on May 28th, the Queen smiles from the cab of CPR 5919, the royal train.

5919

On the Royal Train...

The Royal Train

(Top left) The drawing room where the King and Queen could relax and recoup their energy by talking, reading and listening to the radio. (Above) One of the bedrooms on the royal train. (Bottom left) The royal train moves through the Rockies near Field, B.C. (Inset) The royal train had its own post office, and thus could issue its own postmarks. All over Canada and the United States, people cherished this cancellation mark. One day, 250,000 letters were mailed from the train.

June 2nd, 1939

(Top left) Royal train pulls into Edmonton. For about five kilometres along the track leading into the city, crowds roared approval. About 200,000 people gathered in the city, including hundreds from Peace River country and miners who had flown down from the north.

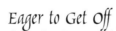

A Periscope for a Better View

(Middle left) On May 19th, the pilot train pulls into Ottawa. At right, a young man is trying out his Dominion Periscope. The building at right is the Ottawa Artificial Ice Company, which supplied ice to Ottawa ice boxes throughout the hot summers.

Eager to Get Off

(Bottom left) On May 26th, at the Calgary CPR station, the royal train pulls in. Members of the Calgary Highlanders and the Royal Canadian Air Force are lined up to greet the King and Queen.

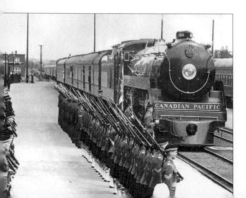

Beavermouth, B.C., May 28th

(Right) Flowers are presented to King George and Queen Elizabeth before they enter the cab of locomotive 5919 for a thrilling ride up the eastern slopes of the Selkirk Mountains.

Waving From the Train

The King and Queen in a typical pose on the platform of their coach. Even if the train merely slowed down without stopping, it still gave thousands of Canadians a good view. On June 6th, about 25,000 people came out to Beaverton, Ontario, to see the Royal Couple.

A Souvenir Coin

Across the country, children placed pennies and nickels on tracks and for years afterward, people prized these coins, flattened by the Royal Train. Here at Kitchener on June 6th, young boys are placing coins on a track in anticipation of the train.

Tour Route

The CNR and CPR distributed this map of the Royal Tour route westward and eastward, set against a view of the Bow Valley, Banff, Alberta.

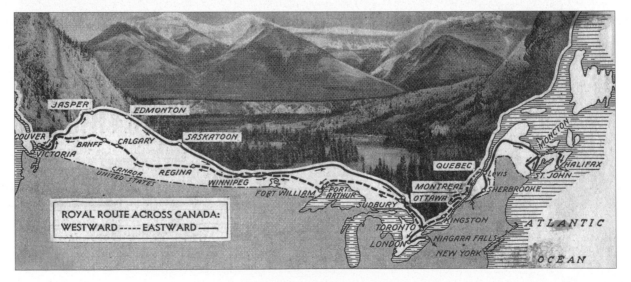

ROYAL ROUTE ACROSS CANADA:
WESTWARD ----- EASTWARD ——

Goodbye to Mount Robson

On June 1st, the royal train pulls out of Mount Robson with the King and Queen on the rear platform and in the distance, the smoke of the engine as the train rounds the mountain.

Arrival and Departure

Heading Up the St. Lawrence

(Right) On May 17th, at Pointe-au-Père, 350km downriver from Québec, the King and Queen on the CPR's *Empress of Australia*. From there to Québec, Augustus Santerre, veteran St. Lawrence river pilot, was in charge of the ship. He called it the greatest honour of his career.

Departing Halifax

(Above left) The King and Queen bid Halifax farewell on June 15th. "You have given us a welcome of which memory will always be dear to us," the King told millions over radio, adding, "*Mon premier devoir est de vous remercier du fond de mon coeur.*" When he finished, everyone in the room was in tears.

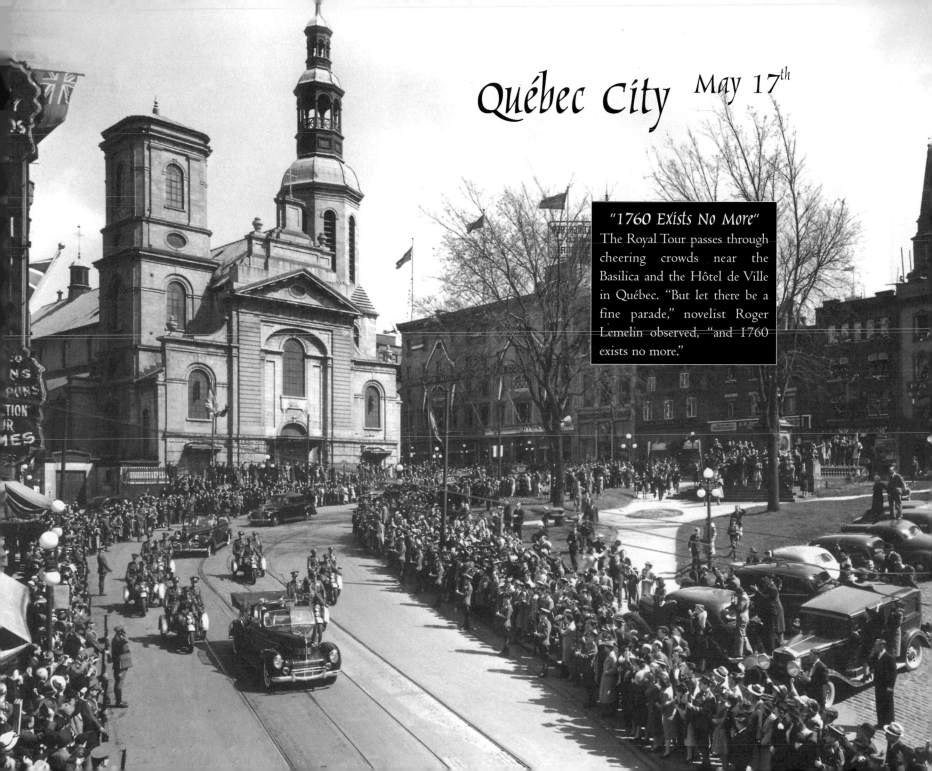

Québec City May 17th

"1760 Exists No More"
The Royal Tour passes through
cheering crowds near the
Basilica and the Hôtel de Ville
in Québec. "But let there be a
fine parade," novelist Roger
Lemelin observed, "and 1760
exists no more."

Québec City, May 17th

Strike Up the Band

The Royal Party drives through cheering crowds on rue St.-Louis. Along the 15-km route, enthusiastic crowds shouted *"Vive le Roi! Vive la Reine!"*

"Dieu Protège le Roi"

On the Plains of Abraham, children sing *"Dieu Protège le Roi"* and "O Canada." Referring to the Union Jack and the Tricolore, the novelist Roger Lemelin lamented the fact that French Canada was "obliged to use the flags of others to achieve a festive air." (Inset) At Québec on May 17th, following in the footsteps of General Wolfe, the Royal Car leaves the dock at Wolfe's Cove/l'Anse-au-Foulon to ascend Côte Gilmour to the Plains above. General James Wolfe took this route in September 1759.

Inside the Provincial Parliament

Church and State officials are presented in the Legislative Council Chamber of the Parliament Buildings in Québec on May 17th. Barely visible above is a large painting by Charles Huot of the first session of the Legislative Assembly of Lower Canada, 21 January 1793.

Trois-Rivières May 18th

50,000 Turn Out

During a brief stop at Trois-Rivières, Quebec, the crowd in Premier Duplessis' home town was estimated at 50,000. "Majesty, the population is at your feet," Mme. Arthur Belliveau, wife of the City Clerk, said to the Queen.

Viewing Montréal

In Montréal, the King and Queen, with Prime Minister Mackenzie King, Mayor Camillien Houde and Mme. Houde, view Montréal from Mont Royal. "Houde himself could not have done better," noted Mackenzie King in his diary, referring to how well Houde had served as host.

Montréal, May 18th

A Special Word for the Queen

In 1935, Mayor Houde had been made a Commander of the British Empire (CBE). Who would have guessed from this photograph that a few months after it was taken, as bombs fell on London, Houde was arrested for advocating resistance to war service?

Signing the Golden Book

King George signs the "Livre d'Or" at Montréal's Hôtel de Ville where five Victoria Cross holders, including Billy Bishop, were presented. The King and Queen were charmed by the ebullient Mayor Houde, beside the King, especially after he reluctantly showed them a piece of paper with a list from his officials telling him what he could and could not do in the presence of the King and Queen.

From the Bottom of My Heart

On May 18th at Montréal's Hôtel de Ville, Mme. Houde presents a bouquet to the Queen. "*Le sourire de la Reine a conquis tous les coeurs*," proclaimed *le Devoir*. The mayor is said to have thanked the King and Queen from "the bottom of his heart," adding that his wife thanked them from her bottom too.

Ottawa
The Capital in Three Days
May 19th

Arrival in Ottawa
As a landau takes King George and Queen Elizabeth into central Ottawa and Confederation Square, the Peace Tower's carillon peals forth a welcome. Officials were concerned that deep potholes on Sussex Avenue would throw them from the landau.

Ottawa, May 19ᵗʰ

Arriving at Parliament Hill

(Far left) Queen Elizabeth emerges from the car before entering Parliament.

Greeting the Prime Minister

The Queen greets Mackenzie King as she arrives on Parliament Hill for the Royal Assent to Bills in the Senate on May 19th.

"Are They Ever Going to Arrive?"

(Page right and inset) In the Senate Chambers of Parliament, senators and judges grow impatient waiting for the arrival of Members of the House of Commons. King George asked Mackenzie King what was keeping them.

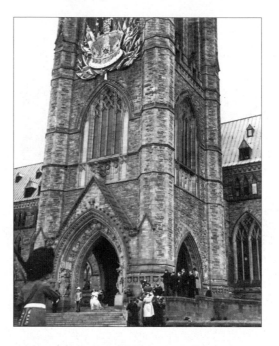

Capturing a Key Moment

(Above) In Ottawa on May 19th, King George and Queen Elizabeth leave the Parliament Buildings following the ceremony of giving Royal Assent to Bills in the Senate Chamber. Cameramen are kept busy at the foot of the magnificent Peace Tower.

The Hartnell Look

(Left) The King and Queen pose for photographers under the Peace Tower. The Queen is wearing a white satin gown embroidered with diamantes and paillettes, one of the many beautiful, ceremonial gowns created by the young British couturier Norman Hartnell.

The Queen's First Speech in Canada

King George and Queen Elizabeth with the Tweedsmuirs and Mackenzie King prior to the laying of the cornerstone of the Supreme Court Building. A Union Jack, then the flag of Empire and the Dominions, covers the cornerstone. She kept the crowd of about 70,000 waiting for ten minutes before she addressed them. Like all good actors, she understood that crowds love suspense. "Perhaps it is not inappropriate," she said, "that this task should be performed by a woman; for woman's position in a civilized society has depended upon the growth of law." In French, she compared the Code Civil in Québec to Scotland's Roman tradition of law.

A Cornerstone Well and Truly Laid

The Queen uses a trowel to lay the cornerstone of the Supreme Court Building. (Right inset) At the cornerstone unveiling on May 20th, the Queen and King chatted with three stone masons, in French and English. (Inset left) The trowel that afterward was presented to the Queen on the occasion of the laying of the cornerstone of the Supreme Court of Canada.

Trooping of the Colour *May 20th*

A Candid Moment

Prior to the Trooping of the Colour, a member of the Governor General's Foot Guards straightens the trousers of a fellow guardsman.

A Fine Place

A panoramic view of Parliament Hill looking south and west during the Trooping of the Colour on May 20th. Later, the Queen told the Prime Minister that Parliament Hill was a much finer venue for the ceremony than the Horse Guards parade grounds in London.

She Loves the Camera

Queen Elizabeth arrives to watch the Trooping of the Colour from the Office of the Governor General in the East Block on Parliament Hill. She always knew where the cameras were located. Apparently the Tweedsmuirs weren't interested.

Royal Garden Party May 20th

Royal Cortège Arrives

The Royal Party arrives for the Royal Garden Party. Yousuf Karsh, who was introduced to the King and Queen, photographed the King in London four years later. At Rideau Hall, Karsh's assistant Madeleine Kindle and her sister Katharine almost landed in a flower bed while curtsying. (Below) Ottawa society is in full regalia for the garden party.

"Like Children at a School Feast"

(Above) On May 20th, at Rideau Hall, the King is surrounded by a sea of wide-brimmed hats during the Royal Garden Party. According to the Governor General, invited guests "cheered the whole time like children at a school feast."

Let Them Eat Cake

May 20th was also King George's official birthday (though the actual day was December 14th). High society in Ottawa, unusually energized that day, lost propriety when the birthday cake was cut. (Below) Serving staff.

Banquet at the Château Laurier *May 20th*

Château Laurier Banquet

(Left) In Ottawa on May 20th, the Royal Couple dine with (l to r) Mrs. T.A. Crerar, Mackenzie King, and Lord Tweedsmuir. Outside, crowds shouted "We want the King! We want the Queen!"

Golden Bowl

(Above) During the banquet at the Château Laurier, the Prime Minister presented the King and Queen with a golden bowl engraved with a map of their route across Canada, fashioned by craftsmen at Eaton's.

Greeting a War Hero

(Right) After the unveiling of the War Memorial on May 21st, the Royal Couple shake the hand of a man who may be H.F.H. Hertzberg, Quartermaster General.

War Memorial   May 21st

Seeking the Best View

During the unveiling of the War Memorial in Ottawa on May 21st, a movie cameraman stands at the ready in front of crowd, as a young man checks his periscope.

Standing on Guard

As King George lays a wreath during the unveiling of the National War Memorial, members of the armed services stand on guard.

The Sculptors

On May 21st, the March brothers, sculptors and designers of Canada's War Memorial, are presented to the King and Queen prior to the unveiling.

Security Breach
In Ottawa on May 19th, as the King and Queen make their way to Lansdowne Park, an admirer breaks through to give his son a better view. The King found the "continuous dinning in the ear" a bit nerve racking. As usual, the Queen is unperturbed.

Scotland Yard Watches

At Ottawa on May 21st, after the unveiling of the War Memorial, a veteran bows deeply while shaking hands with the Queen during the first walkabout in the history of the monarchy. It was the Queen's idea. Up to 7,000 veterans cheered wildly, and respectfully made way for the Royal Couple. "Ay, man, if Hitler could see this," one old vet shouted.

Security

"The capacity of Their Majesties, for getting in touch with the people amounts to genius."

—Governor General Lord Tweedsmuir, 1939

Security Helpless

As the King and Queen depart from War Memorial ceremonies in Ottawa, they are almost lost from view as they stand in their open limousine. A Mountie appears worried at the seeming chaos. Every nook and cranny is crammed with people.

Tight Security

Procession leaves the North Toronto Station at Yonge Street and Summerhill Avenue on May 22nd. The royal salute was fired by the 21st Medium Battery, Royal Canadian Artillery. Rooftops are jammed with onlookers. Although security appeared somewhat casual and merely ceremonial, great care and expense was taken to protect King George and Queen Elizabeth.

Checking His List

In the pilot train somewhere west of Calgary, a Mountie, leaving nothing to chance, checks a list while a cameraman checks his film. About a dozen cameras rest on a table. The photo equipment was state of the art, and included a model "D" Omega Enlarger with a special 30-volt projection bulb, costing $235.00.

Rooftop Security

At Calgary on May 26th, a couple of men stand on the roof of the CPR station. One of the men appears to be an armed soldier; the other, a cameraman.

Careful Scrutiny

At Calgary on May 26th, a Mountie appears to be checking the identity and ownership of a box that may be a cameraman's equipment.

Security For the Royal Tour

Securing the Royals

(Above left) One of the Canadian destroyers that accompanied Canadian Pacific's *Empress of Australia* from the Cabot Strait to Québec City. On both sides of the river, bonfires blazed a welcome. (Bottom left) Airplanes escort the *Empress of Britain* from Halifax on June 15th, en route to Newfoundland. As the *Empress* departed, massed pipers played "Will Ye No Come Back Again." Long after the ship vanished, a great bonfire burned at Chebucto Head.

Canadian Soil

(Page right) A Mountie salutes as Queen Elizabeth sets foot on Canadian soil at Québec on May 17th. Some of the ship's crew watches out of portholes. According to *le Devoir*, it was not long before everyone was saying *"Elle est plus gentille encore, plus gracieuse même qu'on ne l'imaginait."*

Toronto May 22nd

"See Their Majesties From Here"
(Above) Mayor and Mrs. Day welcome the King and Queen to City Hall Square, Toronto. On the south side of Queen Street, a small sign says "See Their Majesties From Here," no doubt after paying a small entrance fee.

At Toronto City Hall
(Left) A huge crowd gathers in front of the (old) City Hall. People hang from the windows of the Ritz Hotel on Bay Street. To the left of the Ritz is the Manning Chambers building at Bay and Queen Streets, named after a former mayor.

The Quints Arrive

The Dionne quintuplets arrive at Toronto on May 22nd with a nurse and Mme. Dionne to meet the King and Queen at Queen's Park. After polite curtsies, Cécile held up her arms to the Queen, who knelt down to receive a hug and a kiss. Always sensitive to public opinion, Mackenzie King was happy that he was booed only two or three times during the day.

Port Arthur May 23rd

Arrival at Port Arthur, Ontario
The King and Queen pay the Lakehead (now Thunder Bay) a brief visit on May 23rd. Member of Parliament C.D. Howe was there to greet them, as well as a flower girl, crowds and cameras.

Winnipeg May 24th

Portage and Main

Winnipeggers wave at the King and Queen as the cortège moves down Main Street towards the famed intersection of Portage and Main. Photographers had a challenging job in the rain.

Winnipeg May 24th

The Umbrellas of Winnipeg
In Winnipeg on Empire Day, May 24th, a sea of umbrellas surrounds the Provincial Legislature. The city's mayor was John Queen, thus making two Kings and two Queens present that day, which so confused a local broadcaster that he uttered a one-syllable word for solid waste.

The Mountie Always Gets His Stole

At the RCMP Chapel at Regina on May 25th, a Mountie holds the Queen's fur stole. Pointing, at back, is Commissioner S.T. Wood. (Inset) A Native encampment was set up at the end of the grandstand. CIL (Canadian Industries Limited) paints received a good advertisement.

Medicine Hat   May 26th

A Sea of People
In Medicine Hat, the King and Queen on a reviewing stand are surrounded by waving Union Jacks.

Calgary   May 26th

A Calgary Welcome

The Royal Car passes the York Hotel, York Café and Gibson's Recreation advertising 16 bowling alleys. People holler from second-floor windows, the roof and from the balcony over the front door. (Inset) Queen Elizabeth chats with Mrs. George Pearkes while waiting for the King to inspect the Guard of Honour at the CPR station.

Calgary, May 26th

Calgary Skyline

The Royal Party drives over the Centre Street bridge en route to Medwata Park. Behind (l to r) are the York Hotel, CPR Station, Palliser Hotel, AGT Building in front of the Palliser, Greyhound Building (Calgary Herald Building), and Lougheed Building in front. (Inset) Three people check out one of the cars of the royal train. Although security was usually tight, it was possible to get close to the train.

Buying Off the Press

At the Banff Springs Hotel the King, Queen and Mackenzie King "buy off" the cameramen with a "photo op" in order to give the Royal Couple a few hours to explore the area with only their own cameras present.

Exit the King

The same photograph, but with King George airbrushed out. It was not unusual for politicians from Mackenzie King to Hitler to Stalin to "eliminate" unwanted people from photographs. In this one, the Queen, *sans le roi*, is giving the Prime Minister her undivided attention.

The Cameramen

Members of the Canadian Government Motion Picture Bureau in 1932, many of whom, such as Frank Tyrell, back row, left of centre, were on the Royal Tour.

The Photographers

Photographers

(Left) On May 27th at the Banff Springs Hotel, a view of the photographers who took many of the photographs of the tour. Later, one of them, Eugene Finn, conspired with the Prime Minister to eliminate the King (with an airbrush). (Below) At Port Arthur on May 23rd, photographers are busy snapping the presentation of flowers to the Queen.

A Human Union Jack

On May 18th, some 40,000 school children gather in the Montréal Stadium in the city's east end. About 1,000, dressed in red, white and blue capes, form the Union Jack. When the royal car arrived, the children sang "God Save The King" in French.

Smile!

Aboard the *Princess Marguerite* between Vancouver and Victoria on May 29th, a photographer smiles for one of his buddies.

RD
ION

ERVICE, WAVERLEY 3636

TORONTO DAILY STAR

TORONTO, SATURDAY, JUNE 17, 1939

STAR WANT A
COST SO LITTI
Give Such Good Res

MAY CIRCULATION 221,

They Brought The Sun With Them, Shining

Newspaper View

(Above) A perfect image of majesty and authority. Taken on June 15th, the King and Queen's last day in Canada, this photograph hit the front pages.

Trick Photography

(Left) The bottom of the photograph—where the King and Queen stand one step up in order to gain height—was cropped out.

Elevated Platform used to Capture an Old Ceremony

In order to get the best view of the Hudson's Bay Company "traditional" ceremony of rent payment in Winnipeg, the photographer, left, stands on a specially constructed platform. (Inset) In front of the gate of Upper Fort Garry, Winnipeg, Ashley Cooper, Governor of the Hudson's Bay Company, pays "rent" to the King in the form of a pelt. In accordance with the agreement of 1670, whenever a reigning sovereign visits Rupert's Land, rent of two elk heads and two black beaver skins must be paid.

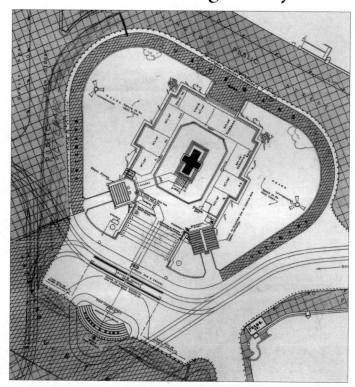

Detailed Planning

(Above) Great care was taken to preserve the visit for posterity. Here is the map made for recording the unveiling of the War Memorial on May 21st. An accompanying note said that windows on the second floor of the Post Office building at Elgin and Sparks were reserved for Captain F.C. Badgley, Director of the Motion Picture Bureau.

On Top of Their Profession

(Left) At Victoria on May 30th, a half-dozen photographers snap pictures of the King and Queen (bottom right) at the Ogden Point Dock before they return to Vancouver. There was no height the cameramen would not scale to attain the best view.

Vancouver May 29th

The New Hotel Vancouver

King George and Queen Elizabeth stop for a luncheon at the Hotel Vancouver, opened only four days earlier. To supervise the events, Manager Joseph Van Wyck, and Headwaiter John Helders were rushed out to Vancouver from Ottawa's Château Laurier.

Sunny Vancouver

(Above) Just as the King and Queen arrived in the city, the sun broke through. Here on May 29th, the royal procession passes over the Burrard Street bridge.

Bird's-Eye View

(Above) In Vancouver, as the Queen waits with Mayor Telford and the Prime Minister, the King inspects the Guard of Honour. A cameraman provides a bird's-eye view of the Seaforth Highlanders and the royal car at the CPR Station.

Native War Canoes

(Left) On May 29th, war canoes accompanied the *Queen Marguerite* as it took the Royal Couple to Victoria. The tallest building on the horizon is the new Hotel Vancouver. Smitten by the area's beauty, the Queen asked about buying one of the Gulf Islands.

Victoria May 30th

The Happiest of Faces

In Victoria, happy crowds greet the King and Queen in front of the British Columbia Legislature. (Inset) On May 30th, a banner welcomes Their Majesties to Victoria's Royal Jubilee Hospital as patients and nurses wave.

The Inner Harbour
King George and Queen Elizabeth against a backdrop of Victoria's lovely Inner Harbour filled with yachts.

Citizens and Dignitaries

Without Ceremony

At Mount Robson, B.C., on June 1st, a moment with Edward A. Hargreaves, aged 84, who sang in the choir of St. George's Chapel, Windsor, at the marriage of the King's grandfather, Edward VII. No previous members of the Royal Family, with the exception of the Prince of Wales (Edward VIII), had been so adept at relating to the ordinary citizens of Canada and the Empire.

How Low can We Curtsey?

Showing Respect
Citizens of Sherbrooke, Québec, greet the King and Queen on June 12th. A graceful curtsey is a little-appreciated art today.

Citizens

An Amusing Moment

(Above) At Mount Robson, B.C., on June 1st, the Queen has a few words with Billy and David.

A Word with a Veteran

(Top left) King George and Queen Elizabeth lean over the rail of a balcony to talk to a veteran at Trois-Rivières, Québec, on May 18th.

Hard Hats

(Lower left) On June 5th, after donning mining attire, the Royal Couple descend about 2,000 feet below sea level into the Frood iron-ore mine at Copper Cliff, near Sudbury, Ontario, owned by International Nickel.

Dignitaries

Distinguished Citizens

(Above) In Stratford, Ontario, on June 6th, the King and Queen receive another group of distinguished citizens. Behind is Prime Minister Mackenzie King and at right, Mrs. Henry, wife of Mayor T.E. Henry.

An Enormous Bow

(Above right) In Toronto, Ontario, on May 22nd, the King greets the Honourable Albert Matthews, Lieutenant-Governor of Ontario, as Premier Mitchell Hepburn and the Prime Minister look on. Despite political disagreements, Mackenzie King arranged that Hepburn's two adopted children be presented to the King and Queen.

Fancy Hats

(Below right) On June 15th, the Royal Couple meet local citizens during a reception at the Halifax station. Opposite the King is the Prime Minister; on the King's right is the Honourable Ronald Irwin, Lieutenant-Governor, and farther right, Governor General Lord Tweedsmuir.

Back to the Mainland ^{May 31}ˢᵗ

Back to the Mainland

On the morning of May 31st, the *Prince Robert*, bringing the Royal Couple back to Vancouver, passes under the Lions Gate Bridge.

A Day Off

At Jasper Park Lodge on June 1st, the King and Queen leave Outlook Cabin for a tour through the park.

Edmonton June 2nd

Climbing for the View

Acknowledging the crowds outside Edmonton's Legislature. Though the Dominion Government had recently disallowed several of Premier Aberhart's money bills, the Premier and the Prime Minister had "real affection for each other," according to Mackenzie King. (Inset left) On June 2nd, Premier Aberhart assures the King and Queen "of the sincere and enduring loyalty" of the people of Alberta. The King rarely replied to speeches of welcome, except in writing. He handed his speech to the Premier. (Inset right) Moments after this scene on June 2nd, the Aberharts and the Prime Minister were left standing outside the closed door of the Vice-Regal suite while Lt.-Governor Bowen and his wife took tea with the Royal Couple.

Biggar June 3rd

Travelling Great Distances

The Queen stands among 5,000 children from Biggar, Saskatchewan, and surrounding area. "There is something particularly appealing about these people of the plains…who have come great distances…" noted the Prime Minister. (Inset) At Biggar, a large banner welcomes the King and Queen.

Portrait of Queen Victoria

At Medwata Park, Calgary, on May 26th, the King and Queen greet Chieftains of five tribes whose ancestors in 1877 signed Treaty Number 7, ceding a huge tract of land to the Crown. Both Calgary and Strathmore, named in 1884 after the Queen's grandfather, the 13th Earl of Strathmore, are located in this tract.

First Nations

"I hold fast all the promises you have made, and I hope they will last as the sun rises and the water flows."

—Mawedopenais, chief spokesman for the Ojibwa at Fort Frances during the signing of Treaty Number 3, 1873.

In Attendance

A British Columbia Native attends events in Vancouver on May 29th.

Ceremonial Attire

Natives from the Prairies and the West attend events in Regina (above) on May 25th, and in Vancouver (left) on May 29th.

Babe in a Basket

On June 4th, Native Canadians wait for the King and Queen at Sioux Lookout, Ontario. A short time earlier, having noticed two women with babies, the Queen returned to the Royal Suite and sent back a box of cookies labelled "For the babies."

Saskatoon June 3rd

A Métis Veteran

(Right) At Saskatoon, the King and Queen welcome Thomas Swain, 104-year-old veteran of the Riel Rebellion of 1885. The same day, Mackenzie King received a telegram from British Prime Minister Chamberlain, congratulating him on the successful tour, which far exceeded government expectations in London. (Above) At the Massey Harris plant in Saskatoon, schoolchildren hold pieces of red, white and blue cloth to form a Union Jack.

In a Wicker Wheelchair
King George and Queen Elizabeth are introduced to a Brantford, Ontario, resident.

St. Catharines June 7th

Suspended Animation
In St. Catharines, Ontario, even Prime Minister King seems at a loss for words while the mayor's wife waits to present the Queen flowers.

Niagara Falls June 7th

At Niagara Falls
The King and Queen take in the beauty of the Falls. Earlier, on Niagara Street in St. Catharines, the royal car drove through an electric light beam that officially opened the Queen Elizabeth Way, the new highway from Niagara Falls and St. Catharines to Toronto.

Washington's Memorial to Canadians June 9th

The Canadian Connection

At Washington's Arlington National Cemetery, King George places a wreath on the Canadian Cross, a war memorial erected in 1929 to honour over 35,000 American volunteers who served in Canadian units during the First World War, among them novelists William Faulkner and Raymond Chandler.

World's Fair in New York City June 10th

"Too Much Geography and Not Enough History"

Mackenzie King's description of Canada takes on new meaning in the Canadian Pavilion at the New York World's Fair on
June 10th. The very thought of so much geography, represented by the map, seems to weary everyone.

Hon: Sir   May 15th 1939

Would it be possible for me to have a seat
with the Veterans Widows in Ottawa — to see the
procession — and to see our beloved King and Queen
pass by. I was a War Widow — my husband was on
sentry post duty on Vimy Ridge May 25th 1916, but
unfortunately he was killed by a German sniper. my
husband is buried in Cabaret Rouge Cemetery France.
I worked as Post woman from 1916 — 1919 in London
England. when I remarried a Canadian Soldier. 38th
Battalion C.E.F. We are receiving Veterans Allowance.
my husband being disabled through War disabilities.
It would give me great pleasure, to be able to visit
Ottawa — and to be with those that have known the
loss of a dear one. Trusting I am not asking too
much. and hoping to hear from you

I remain

Yours respectfully

Mrs F. Casselman.

Veterans

"To you from failing hands we throw the torch"

—John McCrae, 1915

The Face of Loss

At the unveiling of the National War Memorial in Ottawa on May 21st, Mrs. Catherine Lewis, Silver Cross Mother, her face etched in grief, seems lost in memories of her two sons.

A Face in the Crowd

One veteran (centre) looks at the cameraman in Ottawa on May 21st. When the King and Queen arrived at the War Memorial, "God Save The King" was played, followed by "O Canada." The King remained at the salute. Historian Gustave Lanctot claimed that this royal recognition elevated "O Canada," first performed in Québec on 24 June 1880, "to the status of the Dominion's national song."

Vets and Crowds

On May 21st, veterans and others await the arrival of the Their Majesties for the unveiling of Ottawa's National War Memorial, which, according to tour chronicler Gustave Lanctot, was "the most impressive ceremony of the royal visit." (Inset) Veterans hold back crowds in Halifax on June 15th.

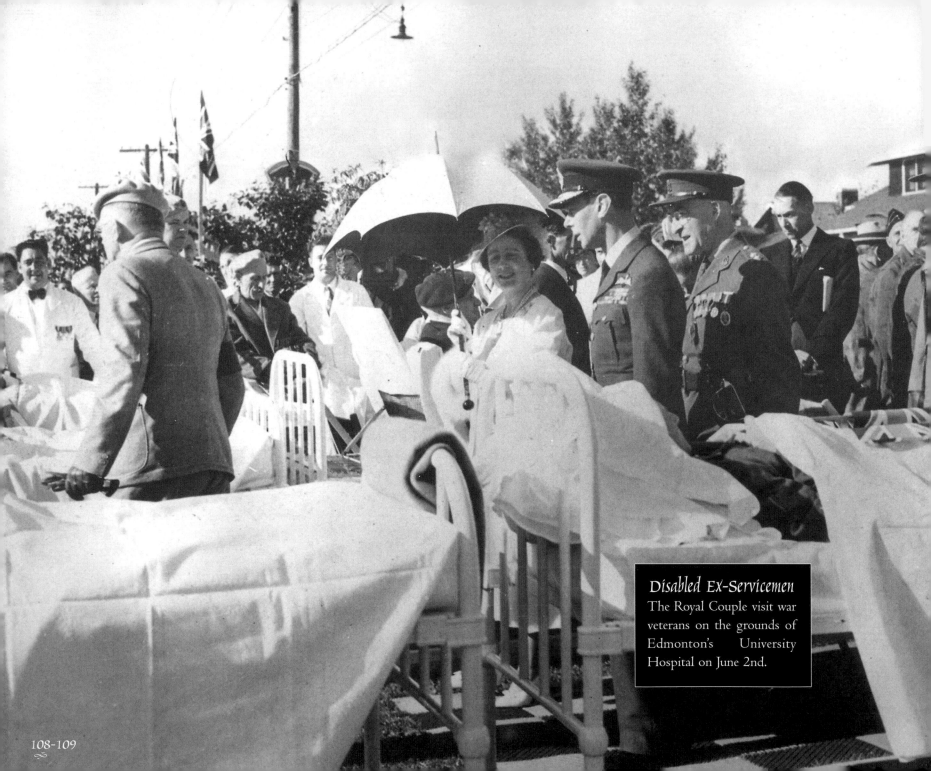

Disabled Ex-Servicemen
The Royal Couple visit war veterans on the grounds of Edmonton's University Hospital on June 2nd.

Spared the Sight

In Toronto on May 22nd, at Christie Street Military Hospital, the King and Queen spoke to bed-ridden patients over a microphone. "I am so sorry," she said, "so many of you are unable to be with us here." They were thus spared the sight of men so maimed by the war that they had to spend the rest of their life hidden in hospital. (Inset) At Ingersoll, Ontario, on June 7th, the Queen steps over the railway tracks to talk to veterans.

Fredericton June 13th

One Mountie Stands Guard

At Fredericton, Queen Elizabeth and Lieutenant-Governor Murray MacLaren watch an inspection of war veterans by the King in front of the Provincial Legislature. At extreme left, a cameraman prepares to capture the event on film.

Saint John   *June 13th*

Happy to be in Saint John
Accompanied by Prime Minister Mackenzie King, the King and Queen arrive at the train station at Fairville, near Saint John, N.B.

The Flower Girls

(Right) The King and Queen always enjoyed unrehearsed moments when ritual and formality broke down. And who better to destroy formality than a child who froze when presenting flowers here at Saskatoon on June 3rd? (Top left) Québec, May 17th. A little girl presents the Queen with flowers while a Mountie stands guard at Spencerwood/Bois de Coulonge, residence of Lieutenant-Governor Patenaude. (Lower left) After this photograph was taken, twins Lily and Betty Dane threw bouquets as the train moved slowly through the station at Beaverton, Ontario, on June 6th. The Queen caught hers first try; the King required two tries.

Children

―∞―

"I shall never forget. We all should be proud that we are Canadians and part of the British Empire, and glad indeed that we have such a good King and Queen to rule over us."

—excerpt from a 1947 grade two reader

Another Bouquet

At Port Arthur (now part of Thunder Bay) on May 23rd, seven-year-old Joyce Evans presents a bouquet to the Queen as Prime Minister Mackenzie King, the Honourable C.D. Howe, M.P., and Mayor Cox look on.

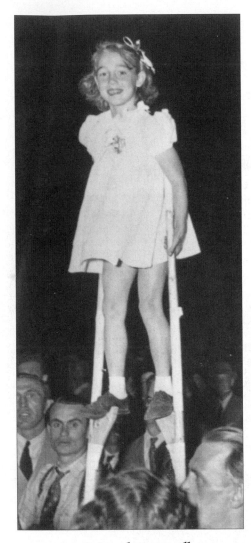

Rising Above it All

At Sioux Lookout, Ontario, on June 4th, Daphine Redding of Hudson solves the problem of how best to see the King and Queen.

Boy Scouts Cheer

Scouts show their enthusiasm for the King and Queen, who, with Premier Angus Macdonald, are leaving Province House, Halifax, on June 15th after signing one of their last registers.

Waiting for the Parade

A veteran and his granddaughter wait for the Royal Couple at Fort William, Ontario on May 23rd.

Capturing the Moment

(Above) Perched on his father's shoulder, a boy in a Mountie outfit waits for the King and Queen on Barrington Street, Halifax, on June 15th. (Right) At Ottawa on May 19th, a young lad seeks shelter while waiting to see the Royal Couple on Parliament Hill during their visit to the Senate. The West Block tower is in the background.

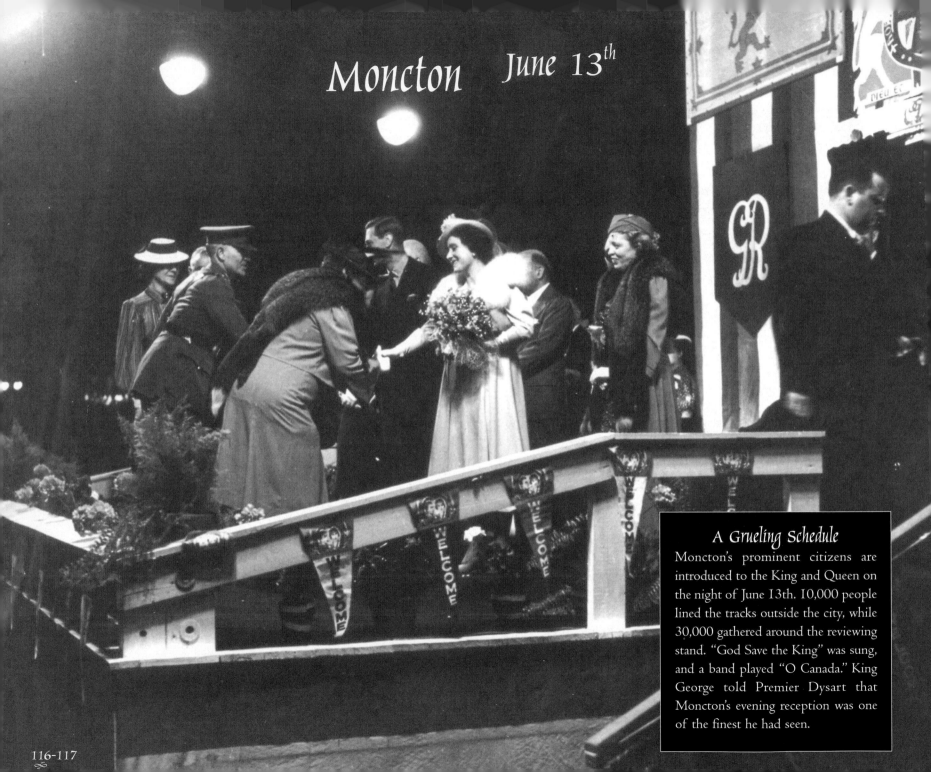

Moncton June 13th

A Grueling Schedule

Moncton's prominent citizens are introduced to the King and Queen on the night of June 13th. 10,000 people lined the tracks outside the city, while 30,000 gathered around the reviewing stand. "God Save the King" was sung, and a band played "O Canada." King George told Premier Dysart that Moncton's evening reception was one of the finest he had seen.

Charlottetown June 14th

Prohibition in P.E.I.

The King and Queen are fortified only by the cheering crowds. King George was known to enjoy a wee tipple...and Prince Edward Island was in the throes of Prohibition. P.E.I. was the first province in Canada to begin the "noble experiment" in 1901 and the last to end it. (Prohibition ended there in 1948, over a decade later than in the other provinces.)

Halifax June 15th

Departure
As King George and Queen Elizabeth leave Canada from Halifax, en route to Newfoundland, a lone Mountie stands guard.

St. John's Welcomes
Their Majesties
On June 17th, the King and Queen talk to veterans and sailors on Water Street. While there, they met Thomas Rickett, holder of the Victoria Cross.

Crowds

Our View of Them—Their View of Us

(Left) At Truro, Nova Scotia, on June 15th, over 30,000 people came to cheer the King and Queen. (Above) Moments later, the cameraman gives us a view of the Truro crowds from the point of view of the King and Queen.

A Motorized Bicycle

A veteran and a young boy pose in a decorated three-wheel motorbike in Edmonton on June 2nd. The scene is probably on Portage Avenue, whose name was changed that day to Kingsway. The King was so impressed by the "splendid sight" of the crowds along the avenue that he personally thanked Percy Abbot, chair of the reception committee.

Capturing the Moment
Students from Bishop's College School, Lennoxville, Québec, getting ready to take photographs of Their Majesties at Sherbrooke on June 12th.

St. Boniface Cheers

While in Winnipeg on May 24th, the King and Queen receive a rousing reception from the francophone residents of St. Boniface.

Crowds Gather

At Glencoe, Ontario, on June 6th, an excited crowd gathers at the station.

Nuggets for the Princesses

Sioux Lookout, Ontario, June 4th. J.E. Hamell holds a gift of gold nuggets for the Royal Princesses.

An Academic Cheer

On June 3rd, members of the University of Saskatchewan raise a cheer for the King and Queen in Saskatoon. In spite of the terrible Depression, no permanent employee of the university was dismissed, though unmarried professors were sometimes forced to take a year's leave with only three months' pay.

The Cast of Characters

On June 6th, the King and Queen have just arrived at the Stratford, Ontario, station. Mackenzie King, who always jumped off the train just before it completely stopped, was ready to make introductions. Here he introduces Mayor T.E. Henry to the King. Out of frame, left, the Queen is descending from the train. This documentary moment captures the tour's cast of characters.

Picture Credits

ABBREVIATIONS

ABT: Archives of Brian Tyrell, Ottawa
ABTEHS: Archives of the Beaverton-Thorah-Eldon Historical Society, Beaverton, Ontario
AS: Alexander Studio, Fredericton
ASN: Associated Screen News Limited
CGMPB: Canadian Government Motion Picture Bureau
CPR: Canadian Pacific Railway
CVC: C. Vincent Collection, St. John's
DTC: Department of Trade and Commerce (Dominion Government)
GS: Gainsborough Studio, Medicine Hat
JM: John Morris, Photographer, Toronto
MKC: Prime Minister Mackenzie King Collection
NA: National Archives of Canada
NYT: New York Times
PMQ: Photo Moderne, Québec
RCGS: Royal Canadian Geographic Society
SW: *The Star Weekly*
TDS: *Toronto Daily Star*

3: NA, PA-211039
4: SW, 17 June 1939
6: NA, PA-209979
7: NA, PA-211156
8: NA, PA-209983
10: NA, PA-209999
11: NA, PA-209857
12: NA, C-148731; (insert) NA, C-148728
13: SW, 10 June 1939
14: (left) NA, PA-211154; (right) NA, PA-210502; (bottom) ABT
15: NA, PA-067248
16: NA, PA-211032
18: NA, PA-211155
19: NA, PA-210498
20: NA, PA-209835
21: NA, PA-211157
23: NA, PA-209849
24: NA, PA-209825
25: NA, PA-210475
26: NA, PA-130524
28: RCGS, NA, PA-210496
29: RCGS, NA, PA-210491
30: RCGS, NA, PA-210500
31: NA, PA-211024
32: ABTEHS
33: NA, PA-130576
34: SW, 10 June 1939
35: NA, PA-210479
36: CPR, NA, PA-210480
37: (upper left, lower left & right) NYT, 11 June 1939; (insert) ABT
38: (upper left) NA, PA-209836; (middle left) RCGS, NA, PA-210481;

(lower left) NA, PA-211035; (right) RCGS, NA, PA-210470
39: ABTEHS
40: NA, PA-209847
41: Newspaper Clipping, date unknown, ca May-June 1939
41: NA, PA-211158
42: (upper left) NA, PA-209993; (right) NA, PA-209827
43: ASN, RCGS, NA, PA-210506
44: (left) NA, C-36289; (right) NA, PA-209824; NA, PA-209822
45: MKC, NA, PA-130395
46: NA, PA-209855
47: NA, PA-211001
48: (left) NA, PA-209997; (middle) NA, PA-211002; (right) NA, PA-209998
49: NA, PA-211009
50: (left and right) SW, 10 June 1939
51: NA, PA-210478; (insert) NA, C-33778
52: (above) NA, C-55371; (left) SW, 10 June 1939
53: (left) NA, PA-130648; (right) NA, PA-210507; (right insert) RCGS, CGMPB, NA, PA-210490; (left insert) RCGS, CGMPB, NA, PA-210503
54: (left) NA, PA-211164; (middle) NA, PA-211011; (right) NA, PA-211163
55: (upper left) NA, C-65500; (lower left) NA, PA-211013; (middle) NA, PA-130700; (upper right) NA, C-33279; (lower right) NA, PA-211160
56: NA, PA-211004
57: (above) NA, PA-210504; (right) NA, PA-211016
58: (left) NA, PA-210486; (middle) CGMPB, DTC, NA, PA-210477; (right) NA, PA-211005
59: NA, PA-211008
60: NA, PA-211006
61: NA, PA-130691
62: RCGS, NA, PA-210499
63: (left) NA, PA-211037; (middle) NA, PA-211151; (right) NA, PA-211038
64: (upper) NA, PA-210472; (lower) MKC, NA, C-85083
65: RCGX, NA, PA-210501
66: (left) SW, 3 June 1939; (right) NA, PA-211019
67: NA, PA-211020
68: NA, PA-211028
69: NA, PA-211031
70: NA, PA-211167
71: NA, PA-211033; (insert) NA, PA-211166
72: GS, NA, PA-211034
73: NA, PA-131107; (insert) NA, PA-211170
74: NA, PA-211036; (insert) NA, PA-211171
75: (left) NA, PA-802278; (right) NA, PA-802277
76: ABT
77: (left) NA, PA-131188; (below) NA, PA-211027
78: (left) NA, PA-130887; (right) NA, PA-211023
79: (upper) TDS, 17 June 1939; (lower) NA, PA-130893
80: NA, PA-211168; (inset) NA, PA-131179

81: NA, PA-211045
82: NA, PA-210508
83: (upper left) NA, PA-211041; (lower left) NA, PA-211152; (right) NA, PA-131191
84: NA, PA-211043; (insert) NA, PA-211046
85: NA, PA-211044
86: NA, PA-131140
87: NA, PA-209858
88: (upper left) PMQ, NA, PA-209826; (lower left) NA, PA-210483; (right) NA, PA-218048
89: (left) NA, PA-209848; (upper right) NA, PA-211018; (lower right) NA, PA-800469
90: RCGS, NA, PA-210505
91: NA, PA-209829
92: NA, PA-130497; (insert left) NA, PA-209830; (inset right) NA, PA-209831
93: NA, PA-209838; (insert) NA, PA-209837
94: NA, PA-131185
95: NA, PA-211040
96: (left) NA, PA-211042; (right) NA, PA-131127
97: NA, PA-130502
98: NA, PA-209840; (insert) NA, PA-209841
99: NA, PA-130545
100: NA, PA-209852
101: NA, PA-209853
102: NA, PA-209854
103: NA, PA-209856
104: NA, C-148721
105: NA, PA-211007
106: NA, C-85092
107: NA, PA-210489; (insert) NA, PA-209989
108: NA, PA-209833
109: JM, NA, PA-211022; (insert) RCGS, NA, PA-210485
110: AS, NA, RD-1039
111: NA, PA-209981
112: (upper left) NA, PA-209723; (lower left) ABTEHS; (right) NA, PA-209839
113: NA, PA-211025
114: (left) NA, PA-209844; (middle) NA, PA-130572; (right) NA, PA-211165
115: (left) NA, PA-209991; (right) PA-211162
116: NA, PA-211000
117: NA, PA-209984
118: NA, PA-209994
119: CVC, NA, C-26498
120: NA, PA-209988
121: NA, PA-209986
122: NA, PA-209832
123: NA, PA-209859
124: (upper) NA, PA-211169; (lower) NA, PA-130529
125: (left) NA, PA-209844; (right) NA, PA-209842
126: NA, C-85096

LYNX⊘ TIME...
LYNX⊘ PLACE ...
LYNX⊘ IMAGES ...

Lynx Images is a unique Canadian company that creates books and films filled with engaging stories and dramatic images from Canada's history.

Lynx projects are journeys of discovery, expeditions to sites where the past still resonates.

The company is comprised of a small, dedicated group of writers and filmmakers who believe that history is something for all of us to explore.

CANADIAN AUTHORS   CANADIAN STORIES

R B FLEMING

Lynx Images seeks out authors who tell Canadian stories in an engaging way. Our talented researchers and writers have created several bestselling books and award-winning films.

R B Fleming is a biographer and historian whose books include *The Railway King of Canada* and *Eldon Connections*. He has written several articles for *The Beaver* on such subjects as Toronto's Yonge Street; Frank Tyrell, a NFB photographer; and Steamboating on Lake Simcoe.

JOIN THE ADVENTURE!

We are searching out powerful archival photographs, film footage, knowledgeable contacts, and stories from Canada's past for our future projects, *Childhood Canada* and *Vanished in the Mist: Lost Newfoundland*. We welcome your input and comments. Please mail, fax, or e-mail us at input@lynximages.com

---

COMMITTED TO A FUTURE OF BRINGING YOU MORE OF THE PAST

Thank you for your support
—Russell Floren, Barbara Chisholm, Andrea Gutsche
WWW.LYNXIMAGES.COM

FROM LYNX⊘ IMAGES

DISASTER CANADA
From the 1700s to Today

DISASTER CANADA travels across the country from its rough beginnings to the present, exploring the history of its most devastating catastrophes. In this book, stories and dramatic photographs expose the human core; our will to survive, our heroism, and our capacity to face the worst. Covers 70 disasters from the 1700s to today. The book also includes a comprehensive list of over 100 Canadian disasters with 200 black and white photographs, maps and diagrams.

288 pages, soft cover, photos & illus.
ISBN 1894073134 $24.95

9 Weeks on the Bestseller List

CASTLES OF THE NORTH
Canada's Grand Hotels

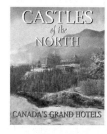

They are Canada's castles, grand historic hotels that are among the country's most recognized and storied landmarks. The hotels were where the country entertained its most distinguished guests—dignitaries, royalty, and celebrities—and they were the place to go in town for afternoon tea or to dance to the Big Band sounds on a Saturday night.

CASTLES OF THE NORTH celebrates this magnificent history. The hardcover book, written by distinguished writers from across the country, features entertaining portraits of the hotels and is lavishly illustrated with 400 photographs. A stunning 70-minute documentary is also available.

ISBN 1-894073-14-2 hard cover (9"x10"), photos $39.95
ISBN 1-894073-15-0 video (70 minutes) $29.95
ISBN 1-894073-16-9 video and book package $59.95

Honourable Mention, Columbus International
Film and Video Festival, 2001